# Chester County
## *PERSPECTIVES*

Antelo Devereux, Jr.

*Schiffer Publishing Ltd*

4880 Lower Valley Road, Atglen, PA 19310

Schiffer Books are available at special discounts for bulk purchases for sales promotions or premiums. Special editions, including personalized covers, corporate imprints, and excerpts can be created in large quantities for special needs. For more information contact the publisher:

Published by Schiffer Publishing Ltd.
4880 Lower Valley Road
Atglen, PA 19310
Phone: (610) 593-1777; Fax: (610) 593-2002
E-mail: Info@schifferbooks.com

For the largest selection of fine reference books on this and related subjects, please visit our web site at **www.schifferbooks.com**
We are always looking for people to write books on new and related subjects. If you have an idea for a book please contact us at the above address.

This book may be purchased from the publisher.
Include $5.00 for shipping.
Please try your bookstore first.
You may write for a free catalog.

In Europe, Schiffer books are distributed by
Bushwood Books
6 Marksbury Ave.
Kew Gardens
Surrey TW9 4JF England
Phone: 44 (0) 20 8392 8585; Fax: 44 (0) 20 8392 9876
E-mail: info@bushwoodbooks.co.uk
Website: www.bushwoodbooks.co.uk

Designed by John P. Cheek
Cover design by Bruce Waters

Type set in Zurich BT/Humanist 521 BT

ISBN: 978-0-7643-3312-5
Printed in China

# INTRODUCTION

The photographs in this book capture bits and pieces of Chester County, Pennsylvania — glimpses of its various features and its historic and present-day character. They barely scratch the surface of what the county offers to the photographer, not to mention the resident, visitor, and artist.

Over three hundred years have passed since the county was organized by William Penn in 1682, and named after Cheshire, England. Much has changed since then, yet in some ways very little has. Remnants, visible reminders of past activities, are intermingled with elements of 21$^{st}$ century progress and growth. Some of the reminders are simply names, ghosts of times past when travel was slow, crossroads mattered and distances between activities were necessarily shorter than they are today. Other remnants are architectural, while still others are found in farming practices and language.

The geographic area of the county was first occupied several thousand years ago by two groups of the Algonquin Native American family — the Lenni-Lenape and the Susquehannas. Through the processes of disease and acquisition of their land by legal and other means, as well as emigration and dislocation, the native population gradually became extinct in Pennsylvania. The last member of the Lenni-Lenape living locally was Indian Hannah, who died in 1803 near Embreeville.

During the early 1600s Dutch, Swedish, and Finnish traders set up outposts along the Delaware River. In 1681, King Charles II granted to Admiral Sir William Penn land that extended east-to-west between the Delaware and Susquehanna Rivers, and north-to-south between the 40$^{th}$ and 43$^{rd}$ parallels of latitude. In 1682, his son, William Penn, arrived and, as proprietor of the Province of Pennsylvania, organized the region into three counties: Bucks, Philadelphia, and Chester. Over time the comparably large land area of the Chester County was reduced to the 760 square miles it encompasses today as neighboring counties, Berks, Lancaster and Delaware, were formed. In addition, when the land grant was made to the Penn family, its south-

3

ern boundary was not clearly fixed and over-lapped with an earlier grant made to the Calvert family of Maryland. Each side laid claim to the land in between. Eventually Messrs. Mason and Dixon were enlisted to survey and establish the line that came to bear their names and forms the boundary between Pennsylvania and Maryland.

During the 18th century, Philadelphia and its environs was the geographic, economic, and political center of the new country-to-be. The city was the largest English-speaking town outside of London, and the Delaware River was the route to the outside world. Chester County's fertile land produced an abundance of food, and its streams and rivers provided energy for mills of all sorts. Rudimentary iron mines and furnaces provided forgings for peace and war, especially in the northern part of the county. Relics of those early years can still be found scattered about the landscape.

With the influx of English, Welsh, and German settlers, growth radiated away from Philadelphia and the river. As a result the county seat was moved west to a small community called Turk's Head, which then, not surprisingly, came to be called West Chester. The relocation of the political center happened with sufficient controversy that the portion of the county closer to the river was separated and became Delaware County. From then on, Chester County no longer had access to the river nor did it share a border with Philadelphia, as do Bucks, Delaware and Montgomery counties. It became, as it were, one step removed from the city. In addition, the pattern of east to west population movement and subdivision is quite apparent, given the significant number of township names that include "east" and "west."

Many of the immigrants to the region were Quakers who followed in William Penn's footsteps. They made a lasting imprint on the county — and indeed on the Philadelphia area — which is seeded with meeting houses, a good portion of which are still active. During the years preceding the Civil War the county's Quakers and other families were an important part of the Underground Railroad, harboring and guiding slaves as they fled from the South. Not to be forgotten are the Mennonites and Amish, German and Swiss-German settlers. Their language and religious and farming practices remain as part of the county's culture.

Today the natural character of Chester County is varied, with wooded hills and valleys in the north, and open fields and valleys in the south and west, all connected by streams and riv-

ers. The human imprint on the county offers extremes of land uses — from dense suburban development on its eastern edge along the Schuylkill River to rural farms on its western edge along the Octoraro River. There are contrasts — high-rise buildings and log houses, shopping malls and general stores, high-speed, divided highways and dirt roads, speeding cars and Amish carriages. While agriculture, mills, and iron forging were part of the colony's, and the young nation's, breadbasket and industrial base, steel and other manufacturing industries have declined and been replaced by various high technology enterprises. Agriculture continues to remain a major part of the county's economy, especially with the advent of mushroom farming. As a result of successful and determined efforts to maintain open space and save land from development, a significant portion of the county also remains relatively undeveloped, considering its proximity to Philadelphia.

# Chester County

## *PERSPECTIVES*

**Valley Forge National Historic Park**
A statue of Revolutionary War hero General Anthony Wayne looks toward Chester County where he was born in nearby Waynesborough.

**Valley Forge National Historic Park**

**Tredyffrin Towship
Knox-Valley Forge
Dam covered bridge**

**Tredyffrin Township**
Diamond Rock School. The octagonal
plan was a popular form of school con-
struction in the early 19th century. Multiple
grades could be taught individually and
supervised collectively.

*Opposite page:*
**Valley Forge**
Freedom Foundation,
Valley Forge

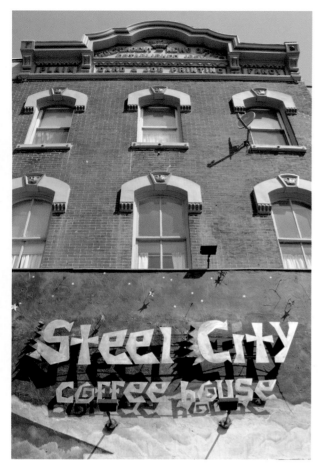

**Phoenixville**
Originally called Manovan, Phoenixville owes its growth to its waterways — the Schulkill River for transportation and the fast-moving French Creek for mill-power.

**Phoenixville**
The town was the location of the Phoenix Iron Works and the well-known Etruscan Majolica pottery made by Griffen, Smith and Hill.

**Phoenixville**
The Reading Railroad bridge
spans the Schuylkill River,

**Schuylkill Township**
Rapps Dam Covered Bridge across French Creek

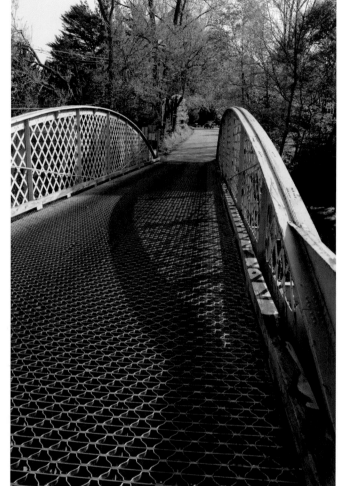

**Kimberton, Schuylkill Township**
Historically significant Hare's Hill Road Bridge was constructed in 1869.

**West Vincent Township**
French Creek

**Birchrunville**
The Birchrunville General Store offers convenience shopping the old-fashioned way.

**Yellow Springs, West Pikeland Township**
The Washington Building dates back to the early 18th century when Yellow Springs was a spa built around its several mineral springs.

**North Coventry Township**
Cedarville United Methodist
Church and Farmers Union.

**Coventryville, South Coventry
Township**

**St. Peter's, Warwick Township**
French Creek

**St. Peter's Village, Warwick Township**
St Peter's Village is on the National Register of Historic Places and is located on French Creek in Warwick Township. It was a late 19$^{th}$ century industrial company village, which served iron mining and granite quarrying businesses. The St. Peter's Inn was the first building erected.

**Warwick County Park, Warwick Township**
Poplar trees. Warwick Township was carved out of Nantmeal and named for the Warwick Iron Works that were within its boundaries.

**Warwick Township**

**Warwick Township**

**East Nantmeal Township**
Nantmeal, which means "sweet water," was settled by Quakers who migrated from Nantmel in Wales.

**East Pikeland Township**
St. Peter's Church. Pike's Land was the first name given to a grant of 10,000 acres by William Penn to Joseph Pike from County Cork, Ireland in 1705.

**East Nantmeal Township**

**West Nantmeal Township**
St. Mary's of Providence. The mansion was built by Joseph D. Potts in the late 19th century and now serves as a retreat for senior citizens.

**West Nantmeal Township**
Isabella Furnace. The remains of iron works owned by Joseph D. Potts. There were several furnaces or forges in northern Chester County which supplied iron to the new and growing country.

### Honey Brook Township
Honey Brook derives its name from Nantmeal, "sweet water." The township surrounds the village of Honey Brook, which sits on a ridge between the headwaters of the east and west branches of the Brandywine River. The village was originally called Waynesburg but had to change its name to avoid railroad freight from being erroneously delivered to the town of Waynesburg in western Pennsylvania.

**Honey Brook Township**
The honor system prevails. Produce for sale at an Amish farm.

**West Nantmeal Township**

**Compass, West Caln Township**
St. John's Church

### Elverson

From the 1850s until the 1930s Elverson was one of the principal commercial centers of northwestern Chester County. The village was established to take advantage of three springs located along the principal trade route between Lancaster and the French Creek iron industries. Accordingly it was originally named Springfield but was renamed Elverson in honor of the owner/ publisher of the *Philadelphia Inquirer,* James Elverson, Sr.

**East Brandywine Township**
A spring house

**West Brandywine Township**
Forks of the Brandywine
Presbyterian Church

27

**West Caln Township**
Hibernia Mansion,
Hibernia County Park

**West Caln Township**
Fiddler's Picnic, Hibernia
County Park

**Coatesville**
Steel mills. The borough is situated on the Brandywine River, at the site of a native American village. It is named after Moses Coates, a prosperous farmer who purchased the land that comprises the center of town in 1787. It has been the site of steel making since 1810.

**Coatesville**
A rare visit by a B-17 to G.O. Carlson Airport.

**East Fallowfield Township**
The Fallowfields (East and West) take their names from Launcelot Fallowfield who came from England and purchased the land from William Penn.

**Highland Township**

**Upper Uwchlan Township**
Marsh Creek State Park.
Uwchlan means "land
above the valley."

**Wallace
Township**
Fairview
Presbyterian
Church

**Wallace Township**
Springton Manor Farm. Formerly the Manor of Springton it is now a county park.

**Embreeville, Newlin Township**

**Newlin Township**
Stargazer's stone. The Stargazers Stone was set in 1764 by Messrs. Mason and Dixon and marks an important astronomical observation point for setting the latitude of their famous line 15 miles to the south.

**Embreeville, Newlin Township**
Bridging the Brandywine

**Marshallton, West Bradford Township**
Bradford Friends Meeting

**Marshallton, West Bradford Township**
Four Dogs Tavern

### Downingtown

The town was originally named Milltown as a reflection of the number of mills which lined Brandywine Creek. Around the time of the American Revolution, Milltown became more commonly known as Downing's Town, because Thomas Downing, a 1717 Quaker immigrant from Bradninch, Devon, England, owned a number of those mills.

**Downingtown**

**West Whiteland Township.**
Whitford station. The seemingly
larger-than-life bridge, which looms
over the Whitford railroad station
along the former Pennsylvania
Railroad's mainline, was part of the
railroad's freight-only Trenton cut-
off to bypass Philadelphia.

**East Goshen Township**
Helicopter Museum, West Chester area

**West Chester University**

38

**West Chester**

**West Chester**
The area was originally known as Turk's Head after an inn of the same name.

**West Chester**

**West Chester**
Weekly farmer's market

**West Chester**
The Chester County Hospital, the county's first and leading hospital

**West Chester**
Chester County Courthouse. The courthouse, a classical revival building, was designed in the 1840s by Thomas U. Walter, one of the architects for the Capitol in Washington, DC.

*Opposite page:*
**West Chester**
Everhart Park

**East Whiteland Township**
Immaculata College. The name Whiteland was brought by Welsh settlers from the Whiteland Gardens, in Flintshire, Wales. In contrast Native Americans called the area "The Dark Valley" because of the numerous trees and undergrowth.

**Historic Sugartown, Willistown Township**
This small village was originally called "Shugart Town" after the owner of an early tavern.

**Westtown Township**
Oakbourne Park. Oakbourne Mansion's idiosyncratic water tower. Oakbourne Mansion was built by Mr. and Mrs. John Hulme in the latter part of the 19th century.

**Malvern**
Paoli Massacre Memorial. On September 21, 1777, the British, led by Lord Grey, attacked American forces under Anthony Wayne, who were waiting in ambush. In the bayonet attack, 53 Americans were killed and over 100 were wounded.

**Devon**
Originated in 1896, Devon Horse Show is the oldest outdoor multi-breed horse show in the United States.

**Devon**
Famous lemon sticks, Devon Horse Show

**Devon**
Devon Horse Show

**Devon**
Devon Horse
Show

**Wayne, Easttown Township**
Historic Waynesborough, homestead of General Anthony

**Easttown Township**
St David's Church

**Dilworthtown, Birmingham Township**
Dilworthtown is on the National Register of Historic Places. During the American Revolution, the town and surrounding area was the scene of the most vigorous fighting of the Battle of Brandywine, September 11, 1777. Dilworthtown was severely damaged by marauding British troops.

**Birmingham Township.**
Lafayette Birmingham Cemetery. The township was named by settlers from Birmingham, England, and organized in 1686. Many of those killed during the Battle of the Brandywine are buried here.

**Birmingham**
Birmingham Friends Meeting. The Birmingham Friends Meeting house was used as a hospital during the Battle of the Brandywine in 1777 as was the nearby Dilworthtown Inn.

49

**Westtown Township**
Church of the Loving Shepherd. A barn becomes a church.

Birmingham Township

**Birmingham Township**
Winter comes in spring. Movie set for "Marley and Me."

**Pocopson Township**
Reading Railroad's Pocopson station.

**East Marlborough Township**
Monument commemorating Indian Hannah, the last Lenape Native American to live in the area.

**East Marlborough Township**
*Longwood Gardens*

**East Marlborough Township**
Longwood Gardens

**East Marlborough Township**
Longwood Gardens

**Kennett Square**
Annual Cinco de Mayo celebration.

### Kennett Square
Mushroom Festival. William Swayne generally is credited with introducing mushroom growing to the area. Around 1885 he wanted to make use of the wasted space under his elevated beds; and so he imported spawn from Europe and began experimenting with mushroom cultivation.

### Kennett Square
Memorial Day Parade. The town was originally called "Kennet" after a village in Wiltshire, England, from where one of the founders, Francis Smith, hailed. Many prominent citizens in and around the town helped slaves escape via the Underground Railroad.

**Kennett Square**
Reservations for dinner here must be made a year in advance.

**Kennett Square,**
The "mushroom capital of the world." Chester County mushroom producers are Pennsylvania's and the nation's leaders. The 2002 census report indicated that Chester County accounted for 37 percent of total U.S. production.

**Kennett Square**
Royal Trumpet mushrooms growing at Phillips Mushroom Farms, the largest grower of specialty mushrooms in the U.S.

**East Marlborough Township**
Cedarcroft, the Bayard Taylor
residence, National Register of
Historic Places

**Kennett Square**
Anson Nixon Park

**New Garden Township**
New Garden Airfield's
annual air show.

**London Grove Township**
Stroud Water Research Center, a
world-class organization devoted
to the study of streams and rivers
nationally and internationally.

**West Marlborough Township**
London Grove Meeting House. A plaque on this white oak tree reads: "This tree was living when William Penn came to Pennsylvania in 1682." In 2007 the "Penn oak tree" was over 325 years old and still going strong.

London Grove Township

London Grove
Township

**New Garden Township**
Brandywine Polo Club

**East Marlborough Township**
Willowdale Steeplechase

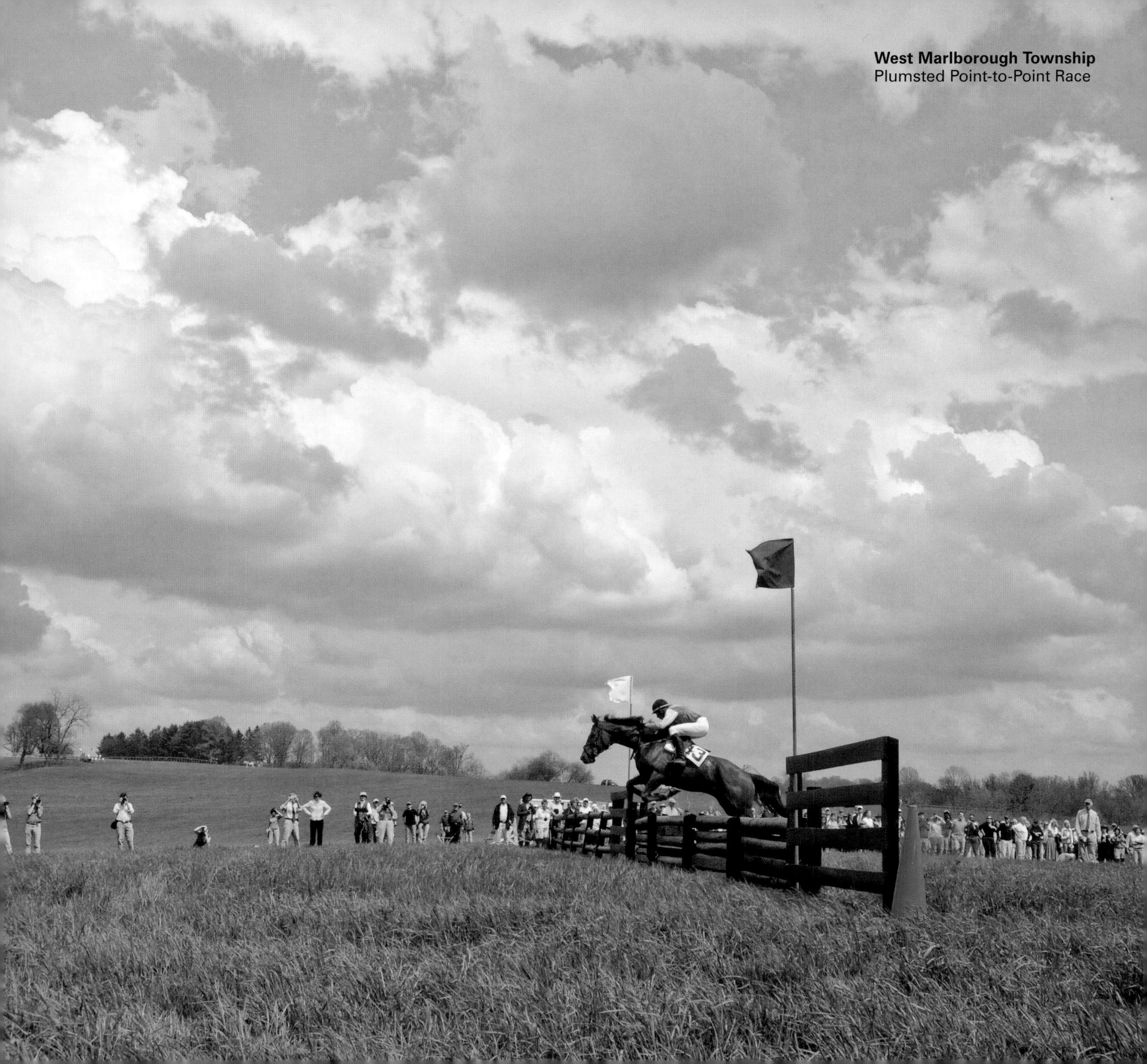

**West Marlborough Township**
Plumsted Point-to-Point Race

**London Grove
Township**

**London Grove Township**
Laurels Driving Event

**East Marlborough Township**
Dog agility competition

**West Marlborough Township**
Fox hunting with Cheshire Hounds

**London Grove Township**

**West Marlborough Township**
Former King Ranch land

71

**West Marlborough Township**
Free range turkeys, Inverbrook
Farm

**West Marlborough Township**
A few among many thousands
of Holstein cows that populate
Chester County

**West Marlborough Township**
Former school house

**West Marlborough Township**
The 4th Continental Light Dragoons encampment at Primitive Hall, Built in 1738 by Joseph Pennock.

**London Grove Township**

**Avondale**
"2,400,000 tomales served"

**London Grove Towship**
Sunset

**London Britain Township**
London Tract Meeting House. A memoral tablet reads: "MINGUANNAN INDIAN TOWN was located here. The chief, Machaloha or Owhala, and his people of the Unami Group – their totem, the tortoise of the Lenni-Lenape or Delaware – sold to William Penn the land between Delaware River and Chesapeake Bay to the falls of the Susquehanna Rivers, October 18, 1683.

**Upper Oxford Township**
Homeville Meeting House

**Lower Oxford Township**
Lincoln University

**Lower Oxford Township**

**Nottingham County Park, West Nottingham Township.**
Former chrome processing plant.

*Opposite page:*
**West Nottingham Township**
The Nottingham Townships are located in the extreme southwestern part of Chester County and abut Maryland. The original settlers of the area were primarily English who received their land grants from either the Penns or Lord Baltimore. Not surprisingly many land ownership controversies arose here until the Mason-Dixon line was established.